John Franklin Rowe

The Gospel in Type and Antitype

John Franklin Rowe

The Gospel in Type and Antitype

ISBN/EAN: 9783337887292

Printed in Europe, USA, Canada, Australia, Japan

Cover: Foto ©Lupo / pixelio.de

More available books at **www.hansebooks.com**

THE GOSPEL IN TYPE

AND ANTITYPE;

ALSO

IN PROPHECY AND FULFILLMENT.

———

THIRD EDITION.

———

BY

JOHN F. ROWE,

(Editor "Christian Leader.")

———

CINCINNATI, 1892.

PREFACE.

This is pre-eminently an age of investigation. Especially is everything of a religious nature probed to the bottom. The Christian is forced to give a reason for the hope that is in him to every one who challenges him. A mere profession goes as an idle tale. Proof and proposition must be homogeneous. We must meet the agnostic challenger upon his own ground, and not shirk the responsibility of investigation. If a thing or an institution exists, there is a reason for its existence. A proposition is proved by testimonies, and testimonies are built upon facts. That which has an existence had a beginning. Christianity has been perpetuated for over eighteen hundred years. Its existence can not be denied. It is either true or false. It originated either with God,

This tract formerly appeared ui der the title "Analogies between the Old and the New Institution. '

or man, or devil. As the devil would not
originate a thing that would destroy his own
kingdom, or man create a system of morals
that would condemn his own practices, so we
must conclude that God himself is the author
of the Bible and of Christianity. And to prove
this proposition, the following pages are pre-
sented to the public as proof indubitable and
conclusive.

THE GOSPEL

IN

TYPE AND ANTITYPE.

No one can understand Christianity, or advance in the divine life, who does not first learn the alphabet of that spiritual system. If he would know something of the knowledge of God, and of the plan of redemption, and of the mission of the Messiah, he must first learn to read the alphabet in the volume of redemption. If he fails in this, his mind will be filled with doubt and distress, and the whole circle of his religious life will be full of shoals and quicksands, and he will float out upon a mystic sea of doubt, like a tempest-tossed ship without pilot or rudder.

God has prepared four great volumes for the improvement and delectation of man; which recount upon their respective pages "the depth of the riches and of the wisdom and of the knowledge of God," and which throw such an abundance of celestial light upon the problem of this life, and upon immortality and eternal life, that even Gabriel and Michael, and Raphael and Uriel, as we imagine, stand around the great white throne, singing and shouting, and adoring, and glorifying the great God of the universe. So limited are the years of man in this state of probation, and so circumscribed in his explorations and investigations, that he is only permitted to read a few pages in these immense folios, which we classify as follows :

The Book of Nature.

The Book of God's Providence.

The Book of God's Moral Government.

The Book of Redemption.

In the Book of Nature, there are heights that can not be scaled ; depths that can not be fathomed ; mines that never can be explored ; seas whose wealth can never be disclosed ; mysteries that may never respond to the touch of science ; latent powers that never can be evolved until the final conflagration. The wise men of the world have turned over a few pages of this teeming volume, and, while reading, they have learned many strange things, have discovered great treasures of useful knowledge, and have gazed upon successive phenomena with wonder and delight.

The Book of Providence is the volume in which we read every day of the goodness and mercy of God—a providence that counts the very hairs of our heads, and that permits not a sparrow to fall to the ground without recognition. God's tender mercies are over all the works of his hands. He sends rain upon the just and unjust, and anticipates the wants of every living creature. In his special providence, we see that he preserved Joseph in the land of Egypt, preserved Moses in the river Nile, overshadowed the infant Jesus in his journey to and from the land of banishment, and sends ministering spirits to the temporary homes of those who shall inherit everlasting life.

In the moral government of God we see that he rules in the armies of heaven ; that he sets up kings in one place and overthrows them in another ; that he " makes the wrath of man to praise him, and restrains the remainder ";

that he punishes the guilty world with war, pestilence and famine; with earthquakes, whirlwinds, tornadoes, monsoons and siroccos; that he hurled down the angels who kept not their first estate, and that he turns into hell all nations that forget his name.

To sinful men the Book of Redemption is most intensely interesting, for it contains that which is of superlative importance to him. In this volume we read of the Seed that would bruise the serpent's head; of the Lamb of God slain from the foundation of the world; of the mission of the Son of God and of his supernatural powers; of Immanuel or God manifested in the flesh; of the death, resurrection and glorification of the Lord Jesus Christ; of his coronation at the right hand of God, exalted to be a Prince and a Savior, Lord of lords and King of kings. We read of the fall of man and of his disgrace, and of his redemption from sin and final exaltation to heaven. We read of sacrifice, atonement, reconciliation, pardon and justification.

The Bible is but an envelope of one superlative idea, of one transcendent proposition, of one personage who is exhaustive of all truth.

Remove the idea of Jesus the Christ from the Law and the Prophets, from the Psalms, and from the altar of sacrifice, as erected by the Patriarchs and' the Prophets, and erase this name from all the types and shadows, and then obliterate this great name from the testimonies of the four Evangelists, and from Acts of the Apostles, and from the Epistolary writings, and from the Book of Revelation, and there is nothing left to contemplate but dry leaves— divinity is withdrawn, the essence of eternal life is absorbed, and the Bible falls to the ordinary level of any human composition.

We now propose to trace out the analogies of the Old Testament, as they typify the birth, the life, the character and the mission of Christ, and as they illustrate his humiliation and exaltation, his prophetic office, his priestly office, his kingly office, his office as Intercessor, his office as final Judge, the glories of his coming Kingdom, and his final victory over death and the grave. As coming events cast their shadows before ; as the thing molded cor-. responds exactly to the mold ; as the impress of type answers to type, so the historical Christ, in every essential feature, answers to the types

and shadows and prophecies of the Patriarchal
and Jewish dispensation. It all has the appearance of the design of an infinite mind.
There stands before us a spiritual perspective
of four thousand years. So marvelous is the
design, so beautiful is the arrangement, so
significant are the resemblances, and so brill-
iant are the radii pointing to, and centering
upon, one great divine Personage, that no one
dare say that the drama of human redemption
was contingent or accidental, and that the
parts, the scenes and the characters came together by a fortuitous concourse of lawless and
causeless atoms. We find the archetypes of
the Christian Dispensation all through the Old
Testament Dispensation—in the altar of sacrifice, in the blood of the victim, in the priestly
consecration, in the office of mediator, in the
laver, in the table of shew-bread, in the altar
of incense, in the golden candelabra, in the
mercy-seat, in the Shekinah ; also in the persons of Abraham, Israel, Joseph, Moses and
David.

The case of Joseph presents a historical
drama, which is full of interest to the Bible
student, and the analogies of which, as they

apply to the person of Christ, constitute a most beautiful study. Witness the following analogies :

Jacob—afterward named Israel, because he wrestled with God — loved his son Joseph more than he loved all the rest of his sons. because of Joseph's superior virtues. God loved his "only-begotted Son" above all the sons of the morning. In him centered all truth and all possibilities of good.

Joseph was hated by his brethren and sold for twenty pieces of silver to strangers—to the Midianites—who carried him a captive boy into Egypt. The infant Jesus, accompanied by Joseph and Mary, his earthly parents, was banished into Egypt, by the infamous decree of King Herod — a decree instigated through fear of the advent of a rival king—then sold into the hands of his enemies for thirty pieces of silver, betrayed by his "own familiar friend," and delivered into the hands of a cruel and relentless mob.

Joseph was thirty years old when he became governor of Egypt : Jesus was thirty years of age when he entered upon his public ministry.

Joseph was repeatedly tempted to do wrong, and the most fascinating influences and the most sensuous allurements were brought to bear on him, if possible to ruin him, but he effectually resisted all the base influences of the Egyptian court and the blandishments of Potiphar's wife. Jesus gloriously resisted the successive temptations of Satan, banished him from his presence, and kept himself perfectly pure and holy.

Joseph was reared in a heathen court, his associates were base men and women, and yet his chastity remained untouched. Jesus was reared from childhood in the country of the Nazarenes, whose inhabitants were so vile and besotted that the fact passed into a proverb, "Can any good thing come out of Nazareth?" and yet Jesus grew up in their midst absolutely without sin in his soul.

Joseph wore a very peculiar coat, which distinguished him from all the rest of his brothers : Jesus wore a seamless robe peculiar to himself.

Joseph was cast into prison, innocent of every crime. Jesus was basely subjected to a mock trial, on charges of crime that were entirely, absolutely baseless.

The Lord assures Joseph of the divine presence while in prison: an angel—the angel Gabriel we presume — assuringly stands by the Savior, while praying and weeping in the garden of Gethsemane.

Joseph proved himself innocent of every charge made by the courtezans of the Egyptian court, and was hence raised to honor and great glory. Jesus was vindicated before men and angels, and then exalted to the throne of God, and made King over all kings.

Joseph forgives his brethren of all their misdeeds, and invites them to come and share with him the honors and wealth and pleasures of his adopted country. Jesus, being promoted to honor and great glory, and coronated a "Prince and a Savior," grants repentance and remission of sins to his betrayers and murderers, and, upon obedience to the gospel, offers the wealth of the heavens to all men.

Joseph never railed out against his accusers, but bore every charge with meekness and godly fear. Jesus, when reviled, reviled not again, but committed his cause to the Father of all righteousness.

Joseph was very forgiving and compassionate, and entertained no hate against his worst enemies. Jesus prayed in behalf of his cruel tormentors—" Father, forgive them, for they know not what they do."

The supreme object of Joseph seemed to be to bless and happify his father and brothers: Jesus "went about all the days of his life doing good"—to his enemies as well as to his friends.

Joseph made himself known to his brethren, after a long and sad separation. After his resurrection Jesus made himself known to his disciples, who, sad and disconsolate, went away from the place of crucifixion without the least expectation that they would ever again see their Lord.

Pharaoh took the signet off his own hand and put it on the hand of Joseph, as a mark of the highest distinction in his court. God exalted Christ to his own right hand in the presence of the Court of Heaven, and addressed him thus: "Thy throne, O God, is forever and ever; a sceptre of righteousness is the sceptre of thy kingdom. Thou hast loved righteousness and hated iniquity ; therefore God, even thy God, hath anointed thee with the oil of gladness above thy associates." "Ask of me, and I shall give thee the heathen for thine inheritance, and the uttermost parts of the earth for thy possession."

As a type of Christ in his various offices of Philanthropist, Savior, Generalissimo, Law-giver, Counselor, King and Prophet, Moses stands forth pre eminent. The analogies between Moses and Christ are as pleasing as they are apposite and luminously striking. There is similarity of relation as well as of life and character. Observe the following analogies:

Moses was the meekest of men; Jesus was meek and lowly in heart.

Moses was the Savior of the Israelites from physical bondage ; Jesus the Christ comes to save the world from the dominion of sin, from its guilt, its shame, its power, and from its eternal consequences.

The infant Moses was found in the bull-rushes of the river Nile and saved from death; the infant Jesus, by the direction of the Angel of the Lord, was sent down into Egypt, that he might be saved from the slaughter of the innocents, as decreed by King Herod. Both Moses and Jesus were providentially preserved.

Moses was under discipline forty years in the land of Midian, before he was called out to go down and deliver the Israelites from the bondage of the Egyptians; Jesus was under discipline thirty years before he was baptized and recognized by his Father, and before he began publicly to teach the people and to emancipate them from the bondage of sin.

The Israelites, as being in bondage to Pharaoh and serving task-masters, are typical of mankind, as being "the servants of sin," and as "serving Satan in sin," and from him receiving "the wages of sin."

"Moses verily was faithful in all his house as a servant, for a testimony of those things which were to be spoken after; but Christ as a son over his own house; whose house are we;" i. e., Christians. Heb. iii. 5, 6.

The letter (the Law) killeth, but the spirit (of Christ) giveth life.

"The ministration of death was glorious," but that which "was glorious" is "done away" from the fact that "the ministration of

the spirit" "exceeds in glory." 2 Cor. iii
8-11.

There are some very clear and beautiful
analogies between the Paschal Lamb, as instituted by Moses, and Christ the Lamb of God,
slain from the foundation of the world   In 1
Cor. v. 7, we find this significant language :
" For even Christ our Passover is sacrificed
for us."

The Paschal Lamb was without blemish ; so
was Christ. 1 Pet. i. 19.

It was killed between the two evenings ; so
was Christ. Matt. xxvii. 45-50.

Its blood procured salvation and deliverance ;
so did the blood of Christ. 1 Pet. i. 18, 19.

Not a bone of it was broken ; not a bone of
the crucified Christ was broken. John xix. 36.

It was eaten without leaven ; in like manner
Christians are required to partake of Christ,
without the leaven of malice or hypocrisy. 1
Cor. v. 7, 8.

At the command of Moses the Israelites
started on their journey. Christ said : " Un-
less you take up your cross and follow me, you
can not be my disciples."

The Israelites started in haste ; sinners. now,

under the leadership of Christ, hasten to get away from the power of Satan.

The Israelites were not to cast any longing eyes backward. Christ said : "He that putteth his hand to the plow looketh not back." "Let the dead bury their dead—follow me." *

Other analogies might be drawn from the Jewish Passover, but these must suffice.

The sanctification of the first-born of the Israelites was typical of Christians who, of their own free will, come out from the world, and set themselves apart to the service of Christ and of the Church.

Cities of refuge were established in Judea to which certain offenders could flee for protection ; sinners now are exhorted to "flee for

* The Israelites were not delivered from their enemies until they had "passed under the cloud and through the sea," and were "baptized unto Moses in the cloud and in the sea." In the institution of the Jewish Passover, here was first the sprinkling of the blood of the innocent lamb, denoting that without the shedding of blood there is no remission of sins; but the Passover was not completed until the Israelites passed under the cloud and through the sea, and baptized unto Moses in the cloud and in the sea—baptized into the government of Moses. So, under Christ, our Passover is not completed until, with the sprinkling of the blood of the Lamb of God, we are "baptized into Christ," "baptized into the one body"—baptized into kingship and government of our invincible Leader

refuge to lay hold on the hope that is set before them in the gospel."

Moses was "educated in all the wisdom of
the Egyptians," and was "mighty in words
and deeds." Of Christ it was said, "never
man spake as he spake;" "even the winds
and the seas obey him."

Moses opened the waters of the Red Sea;
Christ stilled the tempest, and said, "Peace,
be still!"

Moses "refused to be called the son of
Pharaoh's daughter, choosing rather to suffer
affliction with the people of God, than to enjoy
the pleasures of sin for a season; esteeming the
reproach of Christ greater riches than the treasures of Egypt; for he had respec unto the rec-
ompense of reward." Jesus took upon himself the form of a servant; he refused to be
made King of the Jews; "my kingdom is not
of this world," said the Savior of men; he was
not found in kings' houses, but associated for
the most part with the poor and lowly; he refused all worldly honors, and labored in the
flesh for the good of others only.

Moses gave his life for his people, the elect

Jews; Christ died to redeem the world, both Jew and Gentile.

God manifested himself to Moses in the burning bush; He manifested himself to Jesus, the Messiah, by the descent of the Holy Spirit in the form of a dove.

When Moses received the Law through ranks of angels on Mt. Sinai, his face shone with more than ordinary brilliancy, so that he was obliged to veil his face in the presence of the people. On the Mount of Transfiguration, when Christ stood in the presence of Moses, Elijah, Peter, James and John, " his face did shine as the sun, and his raiment was white as the light."

" The Law was given by Moses; but grace and truth came by Jesus Christ."

Moses, in Deut. xviii. 15, delivered the following remarkable oracle concerning the coming Shiloh: "A prophet shall the Lord your God raise up unto you of your brethren, like unto me: him shall you hear." The Shiloh came. He stood upon the Mount of Transfiguration. Both Moses and Elijah were present. Moses was the great lawgiver of a former dispensation. Elijah was the great prophet of a former dispensation. Peter, James and John, who were chosen to be representative men in the coming kingdom of Christ, were present, with the Messiah as the central figure of the group. While standing in this attitude, a voice came from heaven saying: "This is my Son, the Beloved, in whom I am well pleased : HEAR YE HIM !"

The Israelites sought an earthly Canaan : Christians are seeking a heavenly Canaan.

Pentecost means the fiftieth day. Fifty days elapsed from the time the Israelites left Egypt until they reached the base of Mt. Sinai, where they received the Law from the hands of Moses. So, also, fifty days elapsed from the time Christ was crucified—" cut off from among the people "—to the day of Pentecost, when "the law of the spirit of life in Christ Jesus" was revealed from heaven.

When the Law of Moses was promulgated Sinai trembled, and the lightnings gleamed, and the thunders rolled, and the mountain was invested with blackness of darkness. When the Law of the Spirit of Life was revealed to the Apostles on Mt. Zion, " suddenly there came a sound from heaven as of a rushing,

mighty wind, and it filled all the house where
they were sitting. And there appeared to
them cloven tongues like as of fire, and it sat
upon each of them."

The first Covenant was given at Mount Sinai,
1491 B. C., and the second Covenant in Jerusalem, A. D 34.

The Sabbath of the Jews was typical of the
rest (*sabbatismos*) that remains "to the people of God."

As the Israelites assumed Moses as their
leader, being "baptized into [*eis*] Moses in
the cloud and in the sea," so Christians, having "put on Christ " by being " baptized into
him," take him as their only lawgiver, and
his government as their only yoke.

When Moses went down into Egypt, on his
divine legation, he took with him the credentials of his commission. The miracles he performed in the presence of the people and the
magicians were his credentials—visible attestations of his power to deliver the Israelites.
When the Messiah came from the skies, on a
mission of salvation to the world, he also
brought his credentials with him. The wonderful miracles he performed, which were "not

done in a corner," were visible attestations of his supernatural power to redeem his people from the dominion of sin.

The Israelites were willing to follow Moses out of Egypt, because, what they saw in the visitation and infliction of the ten terrible plagues, and in the fact that the rod of Aaron swallowed up the rods of the magicians, produced faith in them to believe that Moses was sent of God, and that he could deliver them out of the hands of their enemies and lead them on to victory.   The people of this world, convinced that Jesus Christ is the Son of God ; that he brought his commission from the Court of Heaven ; that he is an all sufficient Savior and an invincible General, by the fact that he opened the eyes of the blind, unstopped the ears of the deaf, healed the leper, restored the palsied, miraculously fed thousands of people, and raised the dead, and that he himself rose triumphant from the grave—all these ocular demonstrations convince honest people that Jesus Christ is the Son of the living God, and, that being convinced, they have faith to follow where the conquering Hero leads.

The Israelites followed Moses to the Red Sea.

Believing men follow Christ to the baptismal waters. Those who believed in Moses followed him through the parted sea and were saved from the hosts of Pharaoh. They who believe in Christ imitate his example in fulfilling all righteousness, and follow him through the yielding waters of baptism, with the promise of salvation from the dominion of sin and from the power of the Devil.

The Israelites who stood on the banks of deliverance, while the great Jehovah destroyed the hosts of Pharaoh in the depths of the re-surging sea, sang a song of joy and shouted the praises of the Lord. Those who have been "buried with Christ in baptism," "arise to walk in a new life;" and, having overcome the world, the flesh and the Devil, they shout a song of victory over their pursuers, and "rejoice with joy unspeakable and full of glory."

The Israelites who looked upon the Brazen Serpent, erected by the command of Moses, obtained immediate relief from the torturing effects of the physical disease inflicted on them by the fiery serpents of the desert. As an anti-type to this Brazen Serpent, Christ said : "And as Moses lifted up the serpent in the wilderness,

even so must the Son of Man be lifted up, that
whoever believeth in him should not perish, but
have eternal life." "And I, if I be lifted up
from the earth, will draw all men toward me."
Moses saved from temporal death ; Christ saves
from eternal death.

The smitten rock in the desert, and the
never-failing stream that followed the Israelites
for the space of forty years—typical of "that
Spiritual Rock," Christ, smitten for the redemption of his people, and of the blessings con-
tinuously flowing from his pierced side—"a
fountain opened to the house of David and to
the inhabitants of Jerusalem for sin and for
uncleanness."

As the garments of the Israelites never grew
old and never wore out, during their passage
through the wilderness, so the armor of righteousness which Christians are supposed to wear,
is to be worn throughout the lifetime of the
Christian, and to grow brighter and brighter by
every-day use.

The manna on which the Israelites lived from
day to day is typical of the word of God, which
is the spiritual food on which Christians are to
be fed and nourished from day to day.

Joshua, the Hebrew name for Jesus, the successor to Moses, took command of the Israelites and led them to the Promised Land. Jesus Christ, who was "the end of the Law," and who came to "fulfill the Law," having become "the Captain of our salvation," leads the sacramental hosts of God on to victory and to glory. Joshua drove the enemies of God out of the land of Canaan and destroyed their cities. The wicked of this world "the Lord shall consume with the spirit of his mouth, and shall destroy with the brightness of his coming."

"The City of the Great King" was established in the conquered land of Canaan : the "New Jerusalem," the home of the saints, will be established when the Lord comes to "make all things new." John, the Apostle, "saw the Holy City, New Jerusalem, coming down from God out of Heaven, prepared as a bride adorned for her husband."

The land of Canaan was a country that "flowed with milk and honey." Concerning the future Paradise of the Christians, the Apostle Paul says, "Eye hath not seen, nor ear heard, neither have entered into the heart of man the things that God hath prepared for them that love him."

As the Israelites received the land of Canaan as their "inheritance," because God promised it to them, so, also, says Paul the Apostle, God has made Christians "worthy to be partakers of the inheritance with the saints in light," as a fulfillment of his pledge to his people re deemed by the blood of Christ.

The two covenants which God made with Abraham are symbolically represented by Hagar and Sarah, one a concubine and the other the wife of Abraham. The former was a slave; the latter was a free woman. See Gal. iv.

The subjects of these two covenants are, in like manner, represented by the two sons of these two women, Ishmael and Isaac. The former was by birth a slave; the latter was free-born.

The birth of Ishmael was natural ; the birth of Isaac was supernatural. The one was according to the flesh ; the other was by the quickening and renewing energy of the Holy Spirit.

The characters of the two were very dissimilar. Ishmael was a persecutor ; Isaac was patient, gentle, and of a compassionate and forgiving nature.

The fortunes of these two covenants and their subjects are, in like manner, allegorically represented by the fortunes of these mothers and their sons. The former was cast out of the house and family of Abraham; the latter were made his heirs, according to the promise. 2 Cor. iv., and Heb. viii. 7–13.

The covenant of circumcision was typical of the circumcision of the heart under the Christian Dispensation. Its primary design was to separate Abraham and his posterity, according to the flesh, from the rest of mankind, and thus to serve as a sign, seal and token of the Old or National Covenant. And hence it was made a pledge that God would bless Abraham himself, as it was also to him a seal of his justification by faith. Rom. iv. 11. That God would bless all his natural posterity, whether by Hagar, Sarah, or Katurah. That of his seed according to the flesh God would make a great nation, and give them the land of Canaan for an everlasting possession. That through him and his descendants God would bless all the nations of the earth.

Circumcision was made typical of the cutting off of the body of sin from the soul, and the subsequent sealing of it by the Holy Spirit, as is strikingly illustrated by the following Scriptures:

Romans ii. 28, 29: "For he is not a Jew who is one outwardly, neither is that circumcision which is outward in the flesh; but he is a Jew who is one inwardly, and circumcision is that of the heart, in the spirit and not in the letter."

Philippians iii. 3: "For we are the circumcision who worship God in the spirit, and rejoice in Christ Jesus, and have no confidence in the flesh."

Colossians ii. 2–12: "For in him [Christ] dwells all the fullness of the Godhead bodily. And you are complete in him, who is the head of all principality and power; in whom, also, you are circumcised with the circumcision made without hands, in putting off the body of the sins of the flesh by the circumcision of Christ; buried with him in baptism: wherein, also, you are risen with him, through the faith of the operation of God, who hath called him from the dead."

Ephesians i. 13, 14 : "In whom [Christ]
you also trusted, after that you heard the word
of truth, the gospel of your salvation ; in
whom also, after that you believed, you were
sealed with the Holy Spirit of promise, which
is the earnest of our inheritance, until the redemption of the purchased possession, unto the
praise of his glory."

From these passages of Scripture it is evident that the man who was a Jew outwardly
stood to him who was a Jew inwardly, in the
relation of the shadow to the substance, or of
the type to the antitype. That the circumcision of the flesh was a type of the circumcision of the spirit. That the circumcision of
the heart or spirit consists in cutting off from
it the body or the love of sin. That this
is done through the agency of the Holy Spirit,
in the baptism of every truly penitent believer. See Acts ii. 38; Rom. vi. 1–3;
Gal. iii. 27. That the Holy Spirit, as he
dwells in the heart of the Christian, is the seal
of his circumcision. That it is also to him an
earnest of the purchased possession, or a sure
pledge that in due time, if he fail not, he will
enter into the full possession and enjoyment of

the eternal inheritance, which he will share with the saints in light.

Circumcision literally means to *cut around* —to insulate, to confine within a prescribed circuit. The Jewish nation was cut off from all surrounding nations, to preserve them from idolatry, effeminacy, debauchery and licentiousness. Christians are a peculiar people called out from the world (*ek-kaleo*, hence our word *ecclesiastical*), separated from the world, translated from darkness into the marvelous light of the gospel. They are no longer to be partakers of the sins of the world, but to be consecrated to the service of Christ, so that they may be saved from the contaminating influences of the world, and be "made the righteousness of God in Christ."

THE TABERNACLE.

The most wonderful building ever erected
was the Tabernacle. No one can study the
use and design of this building without being
thoroughly convinced that a superhuman mind
conceived the plan, and that an intelligence
superior to man's superintended its execution.
It is the scheme of redemption set up in type.
It is a reflection of the Infinite Mind. It is
the preface to the Gospel Dispensation—the
introduction to the volume of revealed religion.
In its contents we read, by anticipation, the
glories to be revealed in Christ, and discern a
forecast of the superlative beauties of an empire
of love and truth. Manifestly God's purpose
in erecting the Tabernacle, and subsequently
the Temple, was this: that he might provide a
local habitation where he could give a demon-
stration of his presence, and of his power, and
of his glory, and where his people could seek
and find him. See Exod. xxv. 8; 1 Kings
vi. 11–13; 2 Cor. vi. 16; Heb. iii. 6, and Rev.
xxi. 3.

In this wonderful structure were to be found
the symbols of God's presence, the impress of

his divine power, a reflection of his supernal glory. In it we discover a pictorial outline of the System of Salvation—an adumbration of the approaching glories of the Kingdom of God. The Lord Jehovah said to Moses—"See that thou make all things according to *the* pattern I showed thee in the mount." This model emanated from the Infinite Mind. The model was absolutely perfect, and was therefore not susceptible of the least possible improvement. God planned, Moses executed, and the people obeyed. The Tabernacle is variously designated in the Bible as *the Tent, the Tabernacle of the Congregation, the Tabernacle of the Precept or Witness, the House of the Lord, the Sanctuary, the Holy (Place), and the Temple of Jehovah.* When pitched, it always occupied the same relative position to the points of the compass; that is, the place of entrance always stood toward the east, no matter how many times the tribes marched and countermarched, or how often they advanced and retreated. Exposed to the east, the open Tabernacle received the light of the rising sun and the refulgent glories of the eastern horizon. The healing rays of the morning sun illumined and purified the House of the Lord, and penetrated from the east to the west, even as the Sun of Righteousness hath risen in the east with healing in his wings, pouring floods of light upon the dark world, and illuminating the Church with beams of love divine, as he moves from the eastern to the western world—from the Orient to the Occident. As physical light moves westward, and penetrates and illuminates a world of darkness, even so does spiritual light move from the east to the west, penetrating the spiritual darkness of the world and enlightening the nations of earth. As the sun of the solar system sets in the western horizon, and disappears from mortal vision, so the Sun of Righteousness, reflecting the glories of the Christian Dispensation, is now nearing the western horizon of the Kingdom of Grace, and will soon disappear in a sea of glory. And when " the fullness of the Gentiles shall have fully come in," then shall the Son of Man appear upon the clouds of heaven. Then shall the Angel of God's presence stand with one foot upon the land, and one foot upon the sea, and declare—" Time was, time is, but time shall be no more."

The Tabernacle was conveyed from place to place by 22,000 Levites. The materials of this building were all free-will offerings, and consisted of gold, silver and copper, with blue and purple and scarlet fabrics, fine linen, goats' hair, rams' skins dyed red, tachash or colored skins, acacia wood, oil for the lights, spices for anointing oil and for sweet incense, onyx stones and stones for the Ephod. Dr. John Kitto estimates the cost of the Tabernacle, with its appurtenances, at about $1,200,000; the cost of which now, according to the valuation of our money, would in all probability be ten times that amount.

The external parts of the Tabernacle were constructed of heavy planks, made of acacia wood, and covered with gold. Each plank was ten cubits long, a cubit and a half broad, and ten cubits in height. The building was in the form of a parallelogram, the length of it always standing east and west, when set up. There were ninety-six sockets of silver in the foundations of the walls. These walls were supported by five bars made of acacia wood and covered with gold.

The Tabernacle was overspread with four

coverings. .The first consisted of ten curtains
of fine-twined linen. Each thread, according
to the statements of Jewish Rabbis, was six
double; and the entire covering was artistically
beautified with colors of blue and purple
and scarlet, and curiously embroidered all over
with figures of cherubim. Twenty-eight cubits
was the length of each of these curtains, and
four cubits the breadth, and the ten were formed
into two separate hangings of five curtains
each, permanently united together. And these
again were united, when necessary, by fifty
taches or clasps of gold, placed in fifty loops
of blue tape, attached to the selvedges of the
fifth and sixth curtains. Consequently this
covering was forty cubits long and twenty-
eight cubits broad. This curtain of fine-twined
linen formed the interior lining of the Tabernacle.

The second covering was made of eleven
curtains of goats' hair, each curtain being
thirty cubits in length and four in breadth.
These were also joined together in two hangings; the one on the east consisted of six curtains, and the one on the west of five. The

two were united together by fifty brazen clasps.
The first curtain in front was doubled.

The third covering was made of rams' skins
dyed red ; the fourth of tachash skins. The
dimensions of these are not given.

There were two compartments in the Tabernacle — the Holy and the Most Holy Place,
which were separated by a beautiful curtain of
fine linen, similar to the material of the inmost
curtain, the figures and embroideries of which
were also similar. This curtain was suspended
directly under the golden clasps of the linen
curtains, from golden hooks attached to four
pillars of acacia wood, resting on four sockets
of silver, of the value of one talent each.

The entrance of the Tabernacle was closed
by a veil of the same kind of material as the
partition veil. There was less ornamentation
about this. The Rabbis inform us that in the
partition veil and inmost curtain the figures
were made to appear on both sides ; but that
they only appeared on the inside of the entrance veil. This entrance veil was suspended
from golden hooks, attached to five pillars,
which rested on five sockets of brass.

The Tabernacle stood in an outer court.   The

outer court represented a state of nature ; the
Holy Place a state of grace; and the Most
Holy Place a state of glory ; or, the first may
represent the world, the second the Church,
and the third heaven.

The Court in which the Tabernacle stood
was one hundred cubits long and fifty cubits
broad, enclosed with curtains of fine twined
linen five cubits high. The gate of this Court
on the east was composed of a curtain twenty
cubits long and five cubits high, made of blue,
and purple, and scarlet, and fine twined linen,
wrought with fine needle work. These curtains
were suspended on sixty pillars of brass, twenty
on the north side, twenty on the south, ten on
the east, and ten on the west. The pillars
rested on sixty sockets of brass, and were
coupled together above by means of sixty silver
rods, which passed through the same number of
silver hooks.

Here between the Tabernacle and the Outer
Court we find the "middle wall of partition,"
alluded to by the Apostle Paul, separating between the sanctified and the unsanctified—be
tween the Jews and the Gentiles, between the
holy and profane, between those who worshiped

the true and the living God, and those who worshiped the workmanship of their own hands. Hence the line of demarcation was clearly drawn between those exclusively consecrated to the worship of God and those who know not God.

Only two articles of furniture occupied the Court of the Tabernacle—the Altar of Sacrifice and the Laver. Entering the Court from the east (and it was always entered from the east), the officiating priest approached the Altar of burnt offerings, or the Brazen Altar, as it was sometimes called. It was made of acacia wood, overlaid with brass. It was five cubits square and three cubits high. The utensils of the Brazen Altar were all made of brass.

The pans were used in receiving and bearing away the ashes that fell through the grating. The shovels were used in collecting the ashes and cleaning the Altar. The basins were used in receiving the blood of the victims, and in sprinkling it on the Altar. The flesh hooks were used in turning the pieces of flesh, or for removing them from the fire. The censers or fire-pans were used in burning incense Within the boards, and at some distance from the top of the Altar, was suspended a net-work of brass. On this the sacrifices were consumed, and on this the Sacred Fire was ever kept burning. Lev. ix. 24; vi. 12, 13; 2 Chron. vii. 1. In imitation of this Jewish mode of sacrifice, the Persians, Greeks, Romans, and other pagan nations, kept fire constantly burning on their altars. Hence the origin of the Roman Vestal Virgins, whose duty it was to keep the sacred fire ever burning. The Brazen Altar had four rings, two staves, and four horns.

It was at this Altar that God first met with the sinful Jew on terms of reconciliation and justification; hence to every Israelite it became an object of most profound interest, and he approached it with fear and trembling. Here the sinner, by strict obedience to the law, was reconciled to the favor of God in the death of the victim, even as the sinner now, under the New Covenant, is reconciled to God through the death of Christ, who was offered up or suffered "without the camp"; that is, in the world. By faith in the blood of the atonement the devout Jew approached the Altar of Sacrifice; for God, from the beginning, had established this principle in his moral government, that without the shedding of blood there is no remission of sins. Hence Christ, in the anti-type, becomes our Altar of Sacrifice, and to this Altar the sinner comes believing and con-fessing his sins, that through the sacrifice of the Lamb of God, "slain from the foundation of the world," he may be reconciled to God.

We learn from such passages of Scripture as Exodus xxi. 14; 1 Kings i. 50; xxii. 11; Hab-akkuk iii. 4, that the horns of the Altar were made to symbolize divine power and protec-tion. Hence, laying hold of the horns of the Altar means taking hold of the promises of God, through the mediation of Jesus Christ. The fires upon the Altar represent the adminis-trative justice of the great Jehovah. Paul, in Hebrews xii, 29, seems to allude to this symbol of the Old Dispensation when he says: "For our God is a consuming fire."

After the Priest ceased officiating at the Altar of Sacrifice, he next proceeded to the Laver, an article of furniture that stood be-tween the Altar and the door of the Tabernacle. It was a circular basin of brass, having for its pedestal another shallow basin to receive the waste water. In the Septuagint of the Old

Testament it is called *Louter*, from *louo*, to wash, and hence in English it may properly be called a bathing-tub.

Before the priests could enter the Tabernacle they were required, under penalty of death, to wash both their hands and feet in the Laver. They bathed their hands and feet that they might cleanse them of physical pollution. The sinner being wholly polluted with sin, "from the crown of his head to the soles of his feet," must bathe his entire body in the waters of Christian baptism. Notice these allusions in the epistolary writings of the New Testament. There is no mistaking the analogies between the washings of the priests under the Law and the baptism as commanded by Christ.

"Christ loved the church and gave himself for it, that he might sanctify and cleanse it with water by the word"—or, more correctly, according to the Greek, *having cleansed it by a bath of water through the word.*

"Not according to works of righteousness which we have done, but according to his mercy, he saved us by the washing [or bath] of regeneration and the renewing of the Holy

Spirit." Or, according to the Greek, *through a bath of regeneration.* Luther translates it the *bath* of regeneration ; Wesley translates it the laver of regeneration.

"Let us draw near with a true heart, in full assurance of faith, having our hearts sprinkled from an evil conscience, and our bodies washed with pure water." Eph. v. 26 ; Titus iii. 5 ; Heb. x. 22.

As the Laver stood in the Outer Court, and not in the Holy Place, so baptism is an ordinance in the court of the world, and not in the Church. Moses would have been visited with the penalty of death if he had placed the Laver in the Holy Place, or placed the table of shew-bread in the Outer Court. It is to be regretted that in modern times some of the denominations, not comprehending the types and antitypes of Christianity, have transposed the elements of the gospel in such a manner as to produce great confusion. Let it be understood that no one can enter the Church until he has washed his body in the Laver of Regeneration—until he has "put on Christ" in baptism.

The washing of consecration in the ordina-

tion of the priest is also made typical of consecration in the ordinance of baptism. Exodus
xxix. 4; Leviticus viii. 6. In the consecration of the priest the body was washed in
water, and in the consecration of the Christian
his entire body is immersed in water. The
former was to be performed but once, and so
also is the latter. The former was a part of
the ceremony of consecration to the office of
the priest, and the latter is for a similar purpose. All baptized believers are " made kings
and priests to God." The former was followed
by the sprinkling of blood and oil on the person so washed and purified; and it is in and
through the bath of regeneration that believers are brought under the influence of the
blood of Christ, and are made partakers of the
Holy Spirit ; that is, receive "the unction
from above," or, are "sealed with the Holy
Spirit of promise."

The law of cleansing, under the Law, required that the purified Jew, before he could
receive the benefits of the blood of atonement
and appear in the worship of God, must, as the
consummating act in the process of cleansing,
bathe his entire body in water. Without this

consummating act he was rejected, no matter how faithfully and conscientiously he submitted to the preceding requirements of the law of cleansing. If he kept the whole law, and yet offended in one point, he was guilty of all.

Having located the furniture in the Outer Court, and having learned their use and design, let us next enter the Holy Place, which represents the Church of Christ, and note the typical meaning of the articles of furniture found there. On the north side of the Holy Place stood the table of shew-bread, or the Bread of Presence, so called, no doubt, from the fact that it stood in the presence or before the face of Jehovah. This table was made of acacia wood, overlaid with gold. Its dishes for the cakes, its cups for the frankincense, its wine cups and its libation cups, were all made of gold.

Every Sabbath day the priests placed twelve cakes of fine flour upon this table, six in a row, and on each row a cup of frankincense. The cakes were eaten by the priests, and the frankincense was burned. Lev. xxiv. 5-9.

These twelve cakes represented the twelve tribes of Israel, and were typical of the bread

and wine in the household of God, under the
Christian dispensation. They symbolized the
Lord's Supper, and the common priests serving
at that table symbolized Christians, "priests
to God," serving in the spiritual "temple of
God." 1 Peter ii. 5–9.

On the left side of the Holy Place, opposite
the Table of Shrew-bread, stood the Golden
Candle-stick or Candelabrum. It was wrought
out of a talent of pure gold (a talent of gold
being worth $22,500), and consisted of one up-
right shaft and six branches, all ornamented
with "bowls, knops and flowers." On the
top of the main stem and each branch a lamp
was firmly fixed. The snuffers and snuff-
dishes were also of gold. Pure olive oil was
continually burned in these lamps.

What did these seven lamps, which brill-
iantly illuminated this room, symbolize? In
a general sense they symbolized the word of
God, with which the Church of Christ is to be
illuminated, and by means of which the world
is to be enlightened. The three branches
pointing westward represent the Law, the
Prophets and the Psalms, spanning time on
that side, and abutting against the eternity

past; the branches pointing toward the east represent Acts of Apostles, the Epistolary writings, and the Book of Revelation, spanning time on that side, and abutting against the eternity to come; while the center stem represents Jesus Christ, whose history is given by the four Evangelists — Matthew, Mark, Luke and John.

This Golden Candle-stick symbolizes the fact that the Church of Christ is God's appointed means for disseminating the knowledge of salvation, and for dispensing the light of the glorious gospel. This is made evident from such Scriptures as Zech. iv. 1–14; Rev. i. 20. Hence the Church of Christ is fitly represented as a *light dispenser*. 1 Tim. iii. 15. If the Golden Candle-stick itself was only a dispenser of light, so the Church, also, is only a dispenser of light. And as oil throughout the Bible was used as the common and appropriate symbol of the Holy Spirit, so we conclude that it is the Holy Spirit, operating through the word of God, that illuminates sinners and sanctifies saints. This fact will be made apparent by consulting the following passages: Isa. lxi. 1; Acts x. 38; Heb. i. 9;

1 John ii. 20, 27. The seven lamps are symbolic of perfect light. Every Christian is supposed to serve at the Golden Candle-stick in the Church of the living God.

Between the Table of Shew-bread and the Golden Candle-stick, and directly before the veil which separated between the Holy and the Most Holy Place, stood the Altar of In cense, which was made of acacia wood overlaid with gold, and was two cubits in height, one in length and one in breadth. A full description of its use and design may be found in Num. iv. 4-15; Exod. xxx. 1-10; xxxvii. 25-29; Lev. xvi. 18.

Every evening and morning the " Common Priests" offered upon this altar sweet incense, compounded of the most costly and precious unguents. Exod. xxx. 34-38. At this appointed place of prayer and devotion is where God promised to meet his chosen people under the first Covenant, and to receive their oblations of praise and thanksgiving. This incense in the Holy Place was typical of the praise and prayers of the saints in the Church of Christ, under the Second Covenant. As the common priests approached very near the

Mercy seat, unseen to them, when they offered up incense, so Christians approach very near the Mercy-seat in the heavens, though unseen to them, when they gather around the altar of prayer to praise and magnify the name of God. The typical meaning of this incense will be found in Psa. cxli. 2; Luke i. 9, 10; Rev. v. 8, and viii. 3, 4.

The Most Holy Place was impervious to all physical light. Neither natural nor artificial light was ever permitted to penetrate that Sanctuary. As no one but the High Priest was ever allowed to enter that arcanum of mysteries, which was hidden from the vulgar gaze of the people, so are the secrets of the future, or of the unseen world. concealed from the view of Christians who must "walk by faith," and Christ alone, as "the High Priest of our profession," "has entered within the veil."

There was but one piece of furniture in the Most Holy Place. This was the Ark of the Covenant, which was two and a half cubits long, a cubit and a half broad, and a cubit and a half high. It was composed of acacia wood and overlaid both within and without with

pure gold. A full description of it will be
found in Exod. xxv. 10–16; xxxvii. 1–5.
In the Ark were placed the Tables of the
Testimony, the Urn of Manna, and Aaron's
rod. Heb. ix. 4.

The Mercy-seat rested upon the Ark, and
was wrought out of pure gold. On the ex-
tremities of the Mercy-seat, and from the
same piece of solid gold, were formed two
Cherubim with extended wings, and having
inverted faces looking downward and toward
the Mercy-seat. Exod. xxv. 18–22; xxxvii
7–9. Between the Cherubim and on the
Mercy-seat, was the *Shekinah,* or the symbol
of God's presence. It was through the
medium of this oracle that God communicated
with the High Priest, and from the presence
of which the High Priest departed to deliver
the messages of God to the people. Compare
Exod, xxviii 30, with Num. xxvii. 21.

The censers used for burning the daily incense on the Golden Altar in the Holy Place
were made of brass; but the censer used for
burning incense in the Most Holy Place was
made of gold. It was used only by the High
Priest on the Day of Atonement.

The symbolical meaning of all these things
is as instructive as it is beautiful. They were
not only ornamental, but commemorative and
typical. But it is in the typical meaning that
we are chiefly interested. We are indebted to
Milligan's "Scheme of Redemption" for the following order of the symbols and their import.

I. The Urn of Manna commemorated the
miraculous supply of food furnished to the
children of Israel, during the forty years of
their sojourn in the wilderness.

II. The Rod of Aaron commemorated the
rebellion of Korah and God's choice of Aaron's
family for the priesthood. Numbers xvii.
1–13.

III. The Ark of the Chest on which the
Shekinah rested was a symbol of God's throne.
Hebrews iv. 16; Jeremiah iii. 16, 17. And its
containing the Law indicated that said throne
contains within itself the eternal principles of
justice and righteousness. Psalm lxxxix. 14.

IV. But these Tables of the Testimony
needed a propitiatory covering, or otherwise
they would ever be *openly testifying* for God
and against Israel. And hence the great symbolic beauty and fitness of the Mercy-seat,

which, being sprinkled with the blood of Atonement (Leviticus xvi. 14, 19), *covered* the Tables of the Testimony, as Christ now covers all the testimony and demands of law and justice against his people. See Romans iii. 25.

V. The Cherubim evidently represent angels, who have ever looked with intense interest and wonder into the unfolding mysteries of Redemption. 1 Peter i. 12.

As the Mercy-seat of the Israelites was placed in the Most Holy Place of the Tabernacle, so Christ has become a " High Priest of good things to come, by a greater and more perfect Tabernacle "—"a minister of the sanctuary, and of the true Tabernacle, which the Lord pitched, and not man." Hebrews ix. 11 ; viii. 2.

Attention is now called to the numerous and striking analogies between the Aaronic Priesthood and the Priesthood of Christ. After the erection of the Tabernacle, the family of Aaron were made priests to the exclusion of all others.

It was the duty of the priest to offer sacrifice, burn incense, make intercession, pronounce blessings upon the people, and to perform all the services of the Tabernacle. It was also their duty to instruct and guide the people, and to warn and admonish them. Consult the following references to the Scriptures. Exodus xxvii. 20, 21; xxx. 1–10; Luke i. 9; Leviticus i. 5–17; Hebrews viii. 4 and x. 11; Numbers iii. 5–10; iv. 4–15; xviii. 1–7; Leviticus x. 8–11; Deut. xxiv 8, 9; xxxiii. 8–11; Nehemiah viii. 1–8; Jeremiah ii. 8; Malachi ii. 1–9; Luke x. 31, 32.

It was necessary that the priests should not be less than thirty years of age when they began to officiate in the priestly office. After the age of fifty their services became in a large measure voluntary. They were still allowed and expected to " minister with their brethren in the Tabernacle of the Congregation." Numbers viii. 26, and 1 Chronicles xxiii. 27. Every priest was chosen to serve with reference to complete soundness of body and of his intellectual powers. It was required of him that he should be free from all physical impurities, infirmities and imperfections. He was not permitted to defile himself by the touch of a dead body, except in the case of a very near relative (Lev. xxi. 1–6), and the High Priest was not allowed to pollute himself for any one, not even for a father or mother. Lev. xxi. 10-12.

The High priest of the Tabernacle, in his entire personal purity, symbolized the High Priest of the Christian profession—Him "who is holy, harmless, undefiled, separate from sinners, and made higher than the heavens."

The common priest of the Tabernacle, in his comparative purity, symbolized the spiritual purity of Christians in the Church, sanctified body, soul and spirit to the service of Christ, and who are supposed to be "holy in all manner of conversation."

It was also required of every priest that he should not marry any woman of ill fame, nor any one who had been divorced (Lev. xxi. 7, 8), and the High Priest was permitted to marry no one but a virgin of good character and of his own people. Lev. xxi. 13-15. Here, again, we discover some very instructive analogies, which are not accidental, but intentional, as indeed are all the analogies which we have traced through the Bible. As it is certain that the High Priest was ordained as a type of Christ, so it would appear also that his wife was a type of the Church. And the appropriateness of the language of Paul to the Corinthians : "I have espoused you to one husband, that I may present you a *chaste virgin* to Christ." 2 Cor. xi. 2.

The garments of the Priests who ministered at the Altar and in the Tabernacle, were a pair of drawers, a long coat or tunic, a girdle and a turban. These were all made of fine white linen, a sort of select fabric, that, in all the generations past, has been regarded as a fit symbol of purity. See 2 Chron. v. 12, and Revelation xix. 8. Besides these, when in full dress, the High Priest wore four golden garments, viz.: the Robe of Ephod, the Ephod, and the Pectoral or Breast-plate of Judgment.

The Robe of the Ephod was a long sky-blue robe without a seam, and worn directly under the Ephod. Around its lower border were tassels made of blue, and purple, and scarlet, in the form of pomegranates, alternating with golden bells. Exod. xxviii. 31–35; xxxix. 22–26.

The Ephod was a short coat worn over the robe, and, with its curious girdle, was made of gold, and blue. and purple, and scarlet, and fine

twined linen, with cunning work. To the
shoulder-pieces were attached two onyx stones,
on which were engraven the names of the
twelve sons of Jacob " according to their birth."
Exod. xxviii. 6–14; xxxix. 2–7.

The Breast-plate of Judgment, a sort of
pouch in shape, a half cubit square, was made
of gold, and blue, and purple, and scarlet, and
fine twined linen. To each of its four corners
was attached a gold ring, by means of which
it was fastened to the Ephod. On the inside
of its face were four rows of precious stones set
in sockets of gold, through which they were
externally visible, and on these stones was
engraved, "according to their birth," as is
supposed, the names of the Twelve Tribes of
the Children of Israel. See Exodus xxviii.
15–30.

In the Breast-plate were placed the Urim
and the Thummim, denoting *Lights* and *Per-
fections*, or *Revelation* and *Truth*. We learn
from Jewish history and from the Jewish Rab.
bi, that it was by means of the Urim and the
Thummim that the Lord usually responded to
the questions of the High Priest in matters of
high practical importance, involving doubt and

uncertainty. Evidently it was through these media that the Almighty signified his approval or disapproval. See Numbers xxvi 21; Judges xx. 27, 28; 1 Samuel xxiii. 9; xxviii. 6; Ezra ii. 63.

The fourth article belonging to the golden vestment of the High Priest was the Plate of Gold, which was fastened to his Turban by a blue fillet. On this plate was inscribed the weighty words, HOLINESS TO JEHOVAH. The prophet Zechariah (chap. xiv. 20, 21) alludes to this inscription. During the happy and propitious period contemplated by the prophet, everything will be sanctified to Jehovah, as was the High Priest during the Jewish Age. For a description of this Plate, see Exodus xxviii. 36–38 and xxxix. 30; also Psalm xciii. 5.

As the Jewish High Priest bore the Twelve Tribes upon his shoulders, and carried them near his beating heart on the Breast-plate, as he entered the Most Holy Place, and stood in the presence of the Shekinah to propitiate the favor of God in behalf of his people; so Christ, as the High Priest of his redeemed people, bears their burdens and presses them to his sympathetic heart, as he intercedes in their behalf before the Mercy-seat above and propitiates the mercy of God.

The ceremony of consecrating Aaron and his sons to the Priesthood is to be found in Exodus xxix. and Leviticus viii. and ix. We give the order of consecration as prepared in Milligan's "Scheme of Redemption."

I. Moses brought Aaron and his sons to the door of the Tabernacle, and washed them in water. Lev. viii. 5, 6.

II. He clothed them in their proper garments.

III. He anointed the Tabernacle and all its furniture; also the Laver and the Altar; and finally Aaron himself. Verses 10–12.

IV. He brought forward the bullock for a sin-offering; caused Aaron and his sons to place their hands on its head and kill it. He then put some of the blood on the horns of the Brazen Altar; poured out the rest of it at its foot; burned the fat on it; and the skin, flesh and dung he burned without the camp. Verses 14–17.

V. He brought the ram for a burnt-offering, and caused Aaron and his sons to place

their hands on its head and kill it. He then
sprinkled the blood on the Altar round about,
and after cleansing the legs and the entrails, he
burned the whole ram on the Altar for a burnt-
offering. Verses 18–21.

VI. He brought the ram intended for a
peace-offering, otherwise called "the ram of
consecration," and caused Aaron and his sons
to lay their hands on its head and kill it. He
then took of the blood and put it on the right
ear of Aaron and his sons, to sanctify their
ears for hearing; on the thumb of the right
hand, to sanctify their hands for serving; and
on the great toe of the right foot, to sanctify
their feet for treading God's courts. The rest
of the blood he sprinkled on the Altar. Verses
22–24.

He then took the fat, rump, kidneys, caul
or omentum, and the right shoulder, with one
loaf of unleavened bread, one cake of oiled
bread, and one wafer anointed with oil, and
put them into the hands of Aaron and his sons,
and waved them for a wave-offering, and then
burned them on the Altar. Verses 25–28.
The breast he waved and took as his own portion. Verse 29.

He then took some of the blood from the
Altar, mingling it with oil, and sprinkled it on
Aaron and his sons, and on their garments, to
sanctify them. Verse 30.

After that he caused Aaron and his sons to
boil the remainder of the flesh of the ram of
consecration at the door of the Tabernacle of
the congregation. There they ate it with unleavened bread. Verses 31, 32.

VII. The same ceremonies, or at least a portion of them, were repeated for seven successive
days, in order to indicate that the purification
and consecration should be perfect and entire.
Verses 33–36 ; Exod. xix. 36, 37.

VIII. On the eighth day, Aaron, having
been fully consecrated and set apart to the
sacerdotal office, offered sacrifices for himself
and also for the people. At the close of his
ministrations the glory of Jehovah appeared to
the people, and fire came out from him and
consumed the flesh that was on the Altar.
Leviticus ix.

The Apostle Paul tells us that all these
religious rites and ceremonies of the Jews was
"a shadow of good things to come." Aside
from that which was merely of local import-

ance in the Levitical Priesthood, we can not fail to see that an Infinite Mind adumbrated by typical representation, the entire system of Christianity. The sacrifice of Christ, his Priesthood, his Kingship, his Mediatorship, his prophetical office, and his office as final Judge— have all a typical representation in the Patriarchal worship, and in the Tabernacle service of the Israelites. Notice, for instance, the following analogies between the Levitical Priesthood and the Priesthood of Christ.

I. Aaron was called to his priestly office by and according to the pre-arranged plan of God; so was Christ. Hebrews v. 4, 5.

II. The golden letters on the brow of Aaron were a symbol of his entire consecration to the service of God. Christ said, "Do you not know that I must be about my Father's business?" His whole life was one of self-denial and self-consecration. "He went about all the days of his life doing good."

III. As Aaron bore the names of the Twelve Tribes on his shoulders, and carried them near his heart, so Christ bears on his shoulders and near his heart all the heirs of promise. Isaiah ix. 6; Hebrews ii. 14–18.

IV. Once a year Aaron entered the Most
Holy Place, to propitiate the favor of God in
behalf of his chosen people; so, in the end of
the ages, has Christ entered, once for all, into
heaven itself, to intercede in behalf of his
brethren; and to them who look for him, as
the Israelites awaited the return of their High
Priest from the presence of the Shekinah—
waiting "with fear and trembling"—will he
appear again without a sin-offering for their
salvation. Hebrews ix. 28. As the Jewish
High Priest poured out the blood of sacrifice,
to procure reconciliation, then entered the
Most Holy Place to make intercession, and
then returned to the door of the Tabernacle to
bless his people; so Christ, as the Lamb of
God slain from the foundation of the world,
"poured out his soul unto death," that he
might procure reconciliation; having entered
heaven with the blood of propitiation, he now
intercedes before the Mercy-seat in behalf of
his people, and, in the end of all things, he
will come upon the clouds of heaven to bless
his people and confer eternal life on them.

I. The Priests who served daily in the Tabernacle were all types of the citizens of Christ's

Kingdom. Reference is made to this analogy in 1 Peter ii. 5, 9, and Revelation i. 6 ; v. 9.

II. Their white, spotless garments, and their seven-fold washing, were typical of the moral purity and spiritual elevation that is required of all Christians. Revelation xix. 8 ; Hebrews ix. 10–14.

III. The oft-repeated applications of blood and oil signified that this purity of life and heart can only be secured through the atoning blood of Christ, and by the renewing and sanctifying power of the Holy Spirit, operating through the word of his grace. See Hebrews ix. 14 ; x. 16 ; Isaiah lxi. 1; Acts x. 38 ; Hebrews i. 9 ; 1 John ii. 20–27.

IV. The closing festival of their consecration was a beautiful symbol of the spiritual repast of those who have been reconciled to God through the mediation of Christ, who "now rejoice with joy unspeakable and full of glory." Revelation iii. 20 ; Acts ii. 41–47.

V. The separation of the Levitical priests from all secular pursuits, and their exclusion from all carnal revelings, were intended, we doubt not, to indicate that the chief business of the disciples of Christ is to offer up spiritual sacrifices to God in the name of Christ—to offer up their bodies a living sacrifice, holy and acceptable to God, which is their proper and reasonable service. Romans xii. 3 ; Matthew vi. 33 ; Mark x. 28–31 ; 1 Timothy iv. 8 ; 1 Peter ii. 5.

THE DAY OF ATONEMENT was a great and momentous occasion to the Jews. In the celebration of this day were involved the issues of physical life and death—the salvation or the destruction of the people. It was a day of fear and trembling, on account of sin, ingratitude and idolatry. It signified the remembrance of sin once a year. The Atonement took place on the tenth day of the seventh month of the Jewish year. The solemn services were conducted somewhat in the fol lowing order, as we gather our information from Jewish sources :

I.   The High Priest laid aside his ordinary attire, bathed himself in water, and then put on his vestments of gold.

II.   He went to the Laver, washed his hands and his feet, and then proceeded to offer the usual morning oblations.

III.   He went into the Holy Place, trimmed

the lamps, offered the prescribed incense, and then returned and blessed the people, who remained without in great solicitude.

IV. He prepared himself and the people for the more solemn services of the day, by offering the sacrifices indicated in Numbers xxix. 7–11. These consisted of one young bullock, one ram, and seven lambs of the first year without blemish, for a burnt-offering, with their prescribed meat and drink offerings ; and one kid of the goats for a sin-offering

V. He washed his hands and feet a second time at the Laver; next went into the Tabernacle, and put off his golden garments ; bathed himself a second time in water, and then attired himself in his pure white linen garments. Leviticus xvi. 4.

VI. After this he took the bullock, which had been previously selected as a sin-offering for himself and his family, laid his hands upon its head, and uttered the following prayer and confession : "O Lord, I have sinned ; done perversely, and transgressed before thee—I and my house. I beseech thee, O Lord, expiate the sins, perversities and transgressions whereby I have sinned, done perversely, and transgressed —I and my house; as it is written in the law of Moses, thy servant, saying: ' For in this day he will expiate for you, to purge you from all your sins before the Lord, that you may be clean.'" Verse 30.

VII. He then killed the bullock, and re-served its blood.

VIII. He next took a censer full of coals from the Brazen Altar (verse 12. Compare 1 Kings viii. 64), and with his hands full of sweet incense, went into the Most Holy Place, and there burned the incense before the Ark.

IX. His next act was to take the blood of the slain bullock, enter the second time into the Most Holy Place, and sprinkle the blood seven times upon and before the Mercy-seat.

X. Following this act, he came out into the Court, there cast lots for the two goats, that he might know which one was intended for the Lord Jehovah, and which one for *Azazel*, or the Scape-goat.

XI. The High Priest slew the goat which by lot belonged to the Lord; the blood of which he took into the Most Holy Place, where he sprinkled it seven times on and before the Mercy-seat ; and thus he made an atonement both for the people and for the Tabernacle, as he had previously done for himself and his family.

XII. After this performance he proceeded to the Most Holy Place, took a portion of the blood of the bullock and of the goat, applied it to the horns of the Golden Altar, and sprinkled it seven times with his fingers upon the Altar.

XIII. From the Holy Place he went into the Court, laid his hands on the head of the Scape-goat, over its head confessed the sins of the people, and then sent it away by a person, selected for that specific purpose, into a place so deep or remote that it could never find its way back to camp.

XIV. After this he returned to the Tabernacle, laid aside his linen garments, washed himself in water, and re-attired himself with the splendid garments of the priestly office.

XV. He offered one ram as a burnt-offering for himself, and another for the people.

XVI. He burned the fat of the sin-offering on the Brazen Altar, and gave orders that

the flesh and the offal of the slain victims be
burned without the camp.

XVII.   He concluded the entire ceremony
by washing his hands and feet at the foot of
the Laver, after which he proceeded to offer
the evening oblations and to trim and pre-
pare the lamps.

Nothing can be clearer than the fact that
this Day of Atonement—a day of the deepest
humiliation—a solemn season of confession
and contrition—a day when all worldly pursuits were forgotten—foreshadowed Christ as
the great Sacrifice who was to be offered up
once for all, " without spot," at the consummation of the Jewish age, and who was
" manifested to take away our sins."

Look at these analogies between the Aaronic
priesthood and the priesthood of Christ: the
sinner who comes to Christ, comes to Him as
his only altar of sacrifice; comes to Him rely-
ing on the merit of His blood to wash away
sin; comes to Him helpless and hopeless in the
guilt of his own sins; comes to Christ in deep
penitence and humility of heart; and as Jesus
the Christ was baptized in the yielding waves
of the Jordan, that he might " fulfill all

righteousness" and please God, so must the
penitent believer be " baptized into the death
of Christ," be " buried with him in baptism,"
that he may " arise to walk in a new life."
Romans vi. Hence without " the obedience
of faith " sacrifice is of no possible avail. The
two goats offered by the High Priest fitly
represent, as sovereign attributes of God, both
forgiveness and forgetfulness. The goat slain
upon the Altar of Sacrifice represented God's
forgiveness; the Scape goat represented forgetfulness. Hence we presume David alludes
to this circumstance in the 103d Psalm, where
he says, "As far as the east is from the
west, so far has he removed our transgressions
from us."

The Apostle Paul alluded to the veil which
parted off the Holy of Holies, when he said,
" Which hope we have as an anchor of the
soul both sure and steadfast, and which enters
into that within the veil." Heb. iv. 19 ; ix.
11, 12.

To the offerings on the great Altar :

"That you present your bodies a living sacrifice." Romans xii. 1. "I am now ready to
be offered." 2 Tim. iv. 6. And John alludes

to the same when he says, "I saw under the altar the souls of them that were slain for the word of God." Rev. vi. 9.

Paul alludes to the partition wall between the court of the Gentiles and the inner courts, when he says of Christ, "He is our peace who hath made both one, and hath broken down the middle wall of partition between us." Eph. ii. 14.

Scriptural allusions are made to the cisterns under the temple area which supplied water for the sacred rites.

"With joy shall we draw waters out of the wells of salvation." Isa. xii. 3. Jesus stood and cried, saying, "If any man thirst, let him come unto me, and drink. He that believeth on me, as the Scripture hath said, out of his belly shall flow rivers of living waters." John vii. 37, 38.

The aqueduct and subterranean channels leading to Siloam. "There is a river the streams whereof shall make glad the city of God, the Holy Place of the Tabernacles of the Most High." Ps. xlvi. 4. "Waters issued out from under the threshold of the house eastward," etc. Ezek. xlvii. 1–12. "He showed me a pure river of the water of life, clear as crystal, proceeding out of the throne of God and the Lamb." Rev. xxii. 1.

To the *marble pillars* supporting the roof of the temple cloisters, some of them gifts of distant kings, and inscribed with their names. "Him that overcometh will I make a pillar in the temple of my God; and he shall go no more out; and I will write upon him the name of my God, and the name of the city of my God, which is New Jerusalem, and I will write upon him my new name." Rev. iii. 12.

To the foundation walls of the temple. "I have laid the foundation and another buildeth thereon. If any man build on this foundation gold, silver, precious stone, wood, hay, stubble, every man's work shall be made manifest." 1 Cor. iii. 10-13.

"You are built upon the foundation of the Apostles and Prophets, Jesus Christ himself being the chief corner-stone, in whom all the building fitly framed together groweth into a holy temple in the Lord; in whom you also are builded together for a habitation of God through the Spirit." Eph. ii. 19-22.

To the sanctity and inviolability of the tem-

ple. "Know you not that you are the temple
of God, and that the Spirit of God dwelleth
in you? If any man defile the temple of
God, him shall God destroy; for the temple of
God is holy, which temple you are." 1 Cor.
iii. 16, 17. "And there shall in no wise enter
into it anything that defileth, neither whatso-
ever worketh abomination or maketh a lie."
Rev. xxi. 27.

"The first man Adam was made a living
soul; the last Adam was made a quickening
spirit." "The first Adam [the natural man]
is of the earth; the second man [the spiritual
man] is the Lord from heaven." 1 Cor. xv.

"Since by man came death, by man came
also the resurrection of the dead. For as *by*
Adam all die [*en*, Greek, denoting instrumen-
tality], so even *by* [*en*] Christ shall all be made
alive" — resurrected — "but every man in
his own order." Verses 21, 22, 23.

"The law was our schoolmaster [pedagogue]
t) lead us to Christ, that we might be justified
by faith. But after that faith [or a system of
faith] is come, we are no longer under a schoolmaster." Gal. iii. 24, 25. By putting on
"the *new man*"—Christ Jesus and his gov-

ernment—we put off the *old man*—Moses—with the burdensome yoke of the Law.   Col. iii. 10.

Noah's Ark was a type of the Church.   God was long-suffering, "while the Ark was a-preparing, wherein few—that is, eight souls—were saved by water. The like figure [or type] whereunto even baptism doth also now save us (not the putting away of the filth of the flesh, but the answer [or the seeking of a] good conscience toward God) by the resurrection of Jesus Christ." ˙1 Pet. iii. 20, 21.

ORDINANCES.

We can not close our remarks on analogies without saying something on the question of ordinances. There is a disposition on the part of many people, even many religious people, to speak slightingly of ordinances in the divine arrangement, and to regard them as non-essential elements in the salvation of sinners. Persons who take this position may not be aware of the fact that they are opposing their finite will against the infinite will of God, and setting at defiance the supreme authority of Jesus Christ. The chief reason why the Almighty sent judgments upon the land of ancient Israel, and " utterly emptied and utterly spoiled " the country, was because the people, in assuming to govern themselves in defiance of positive enactments, had "transgressed the laws, *changed the ordinance,* broken the everlasting covenant." Isaiah xxiv. 5.

God, by the mouth of the prophet Malachi, recorded the following indictment against the communistic Israelites : " Even from the days of your fathers ye have *gone away from mine ordinances,* and have not kept them."

The Lord arraigns them thus : " Your words
have been stout against me, saith the Lord,
yet you say, What have we spoken so much
against thee? You have said, It is vain to
serve God ; and *what profit* is it that we have
kept his ordinance, and that we have walked
mournfully before the Lord of hosts?" Because of this infidelity the land was blighted
from one end to the other, and the reason of
it was not found in a blind philosophy, or in
the violation of natural laws, but in willful
disobedience to divine authority. When the
infinite God condescends to give to finite man
a reason, philosophical or otherwise, for the
promulgation of positive law, then, as a logical
consequence, man will at once rise to a level
with God, or God must come down to a level
with puny man. Who is prepared for this
alternative? The question still continues to
be propounded by the presumptuous. "*What
profit* is it that we have kept his ordinance?"
We answer emphatically, the profit of a divi-
dend Church, the profit of spiritual desolation,
the profit of ungodliness and worldly-minded-
ness, the profit of increased skepticism and bold
atheism !

We do not intend to argue this question, but we call attention to the following generalization of immutable principles. For instance, man's free moral agency presupposes the necessity of a law above himself; his rationality presupposes the necessary existence of the moral government of God. One is correlative to the other. Law means liberty of action. Where there is no law, anarchy prevails, and in such a community human life is very cheap. Superiority on the part of God means subordination on the part of man. A finite being can not be placed on an equality with an infinite being, nor can fallibility dictate to infallibility. If earthly parents can see the necessity of withholding from their children the reasons of certain things—which reasons they could not comprehend if they were revealed - why should mortal men object because God does not deem it best to explain the reasons for the existence of certain things? If fathers can test the fidelity of their offspring by the alternative of obedience or disobedience to positive commands, why can not God be allowed to test the fidelity of the human family by the alternative of obedience or disobedience to positive law?

Every civil government has its test of loyalty.
Why should it be one particular test, and not
some other—that " would do just as well"?
One test would be just as good as another,
provided it had the sanction of the government. Every government has its oath of
allegiance; but a Communist, who has no law
but the law of self-indulgence, might say,
" What is the use of an oath of allegiance,
since every man is a law unto himself, and
what is the naturalization process but a fig-
ment of the fancy, since all men stand upon
the same plane of absolute equality, and,
therefore, all law is a superfluity?" History
has demonstrated the fact a thousand times,
that bad laws are far better than no laws at all.
But Communism, where there is no law, would
introduce a reign of terror and limitless law-
lessness.

Whenever, in any age of the world, the ef-
fort has been made to govern men or nations
by moral suasion or moral philosophy, or by
the refining influences in literature or science,
failure, alarming and precipitate, followed
fast. No government of any kind could stand
for one day where there is not a supreme,

central head of authority. Of what avail, in the
governing of the Israelites, would it have been
if the Lord had substituted the "reason of
things" instead of his authority, or had tried
moral philosophy instead of the dread terrors
of Sinai? Law implies obedience, and
obedience implies approbation, and approbation implies happiness. This is in harmony
with the law of the mind as well as with all
human experience, and is as immutable as the
law of matter which controls the movements
of the planets. On this principle, God gave
to Adam in Eden, freedom and happiness, by
placing him under a prohibitory law, the
reason of which was never assigned. Adam
had full liberty of action in the garden. Did
not the Lord make a fair proposition to Adam
when he said, "Of all the trees of the garden
thou mayest freely eat, but of the tree of the
knowledge of good and evil, thou shalt not
eat; for, in the day thou eatest thereof, thou
shalt surely die."? Here was the grand test.
Here was permission granted to partake of
everything that is good—food and beauty to
satisfy every possible human desire—as well as
a prohibition not to touch the interdicted tree.

Hence goodness as well as justice emanates from a positive divine law. With Adam it was a question of loyalty or disloyalty. He could choose life or death.

Some writers, quoting from Butler and Whately, use the following distinctions: "Moral duties arise out of the nature of the case itself, prior to external command. Positive duties do not arise out of the nature of the case, but from external command. A positive precept concerns a thing that is right, because it is commanded; a moral precept respects a thing commanded, because it is right. A Jew was bound to honor his parents, and also to worship at Jerusalem; the former was commanded because it was right, and the latter was right because it was commanded."

We do not feel disposed to use these meta-physical distinctions, because they may not be very intelligible to the common reader; but they can distinguish the " ordinances of divine serv-ice" from the Decalogue or moral law. God, in every dispensation, has used ordinances as methods of teaching, and as object lessons, just as the ordinances of heaven—the sun, moon and stars—rule by day and by night. Some men will accept moral law, but not positive law or ordinances. They speak of the latter as being arbitrary. If these critics will examine their own physical organization, they will find a law in their members as arbitrary as a divine ordinance. Medical men tell us of two systems of organs—the voluntary and the involuntary. The voluntary organs we can control, such as the operation of the five senses—the shutting of the eye, the closing of the ear, etc.—but the involuntary organs we can not control, such as the circulation of the blood, the palpitation of the heart, and the various secretions of the juices of the system.

We are also told that there is no virtue in the waters of baptism. No intelligent man contends for this. We might retort by saying that there is no virtue in the blood of Christ to cleanse from sin, as no one has ever seen a *literal* application of his blood. And since it is a fact that water as well as blood issued from the pierced side of the Savior, why is there not as much virtue in the water as in the blood? But as it is impossible to literally apply the blood of Christ, in cleansing the soul from all unrighteousness, we must conclude

that it is *by faith in the blood* of the atonement, and by obedience to the absolute authority of Jesus Christ, that we are reconciled and made the children of God. The
virtue consists in unreserved obedience to divine
positive law. We shall now present a number
of illustrations of this principle of the moral
government of God, taken from the divine
record.

As by the violation of a positive law, sin
was introduced into the world, with all its
concomitants of misery and woe and spiritual
desolation, so by obedience to a positive law
(baptism) in the kingdom of Christ, a sinner
is saved from sin and restored to the favor of
God, who, because of the change in relation,
at once becomes a Father to his redeemed and
adopted children. It was for violating a positive law that Nadab and Abihu, with their
associates, were destroyed. Leviticus x. Because Moses tampered with a positive command,
by substituting smiting with a rod for speaking, he was prohibited from entering the promised land. Numbers xx. Uzzah was instantly
struck down dead for touching the Ark of the
Covenant. 2 Samuel vi. For the violation of

the positive institution, the Sabbath day, the
man in the wilderness was stoned to death.
Numbers xv. For profaning the Sabbath day,
as chief among other violated ordinances, the
Israelites were driven away captives into Baby-
lon. Neh. xiii. 17, 18 ; Ezek. xx. 13–24 ;
Jer. xvii. 27. Many members of the Cor-
inthian Church, by turning the Lord's Supper
into a bacchanalian feast, suffered by disease
and death. This is not now repeated, as a physical punishment, for the reason that the Apostles are not here and miracles of this sort
ceased with their death; but a worse than physical penalty is in reserve as an eternal retribu-
tion for all who defy the positive commands of
Jesus Christ.

Under the Patriarchal and Jewish dispensa-
tions, the person who complied with the positive institution of sacrifice, by presenting his
sin-offering according to the divine decree,
through the word of God, received the fullest
assurance of pardon (even the most barbarous
nations, where the idea of a supreme Being is
almost obliterated, recognize the necessity of
sacrifice and expiation). Compliance with the
positive rite of circumcision entitled the Israel-

ite to the privileges and immunities of the
Jewish Commonwealth. It was in complying
with a positive institution—*by faith* turning
their eyes toward the brazen serpent—that the
rebellious Israelites, bitten by fiery serpents in
the wilderness, were cured of the terrible effects of the serpent's bite. Numbers xxi. Was
there any virtue in the fact that Naaman, the
Syrian captain, was healed of his leprosy by
dipping his person seven times in the waters of
the Jordan? If the prophet of the Lord had
suspended his cure on one act of dipping,
would not the effect have been the same?
Why? Because he obeyed authority and ex-
ercised faith in the words of him who spoke.
The Lord said to Joshua, when he was besieging
Jericho, that if he would march his army around
the walls of the city for seven successive days,
blowing rams' horns, and on the seventh day
march around seven times, blowing rams' horns
and closing the march with a triumphant shout,
he would cause the walls to fall apart in an in-
stant and tumble to the ground. Who says
there was any virtue in rams' horns? No-
body of any sense. The virtue was in obedience to a positive demand. When the pass-

over was instituted, when the Israelites were about to flee from Egypt, why was it, that wherever the blood of the sacrificial lamb was smeared on the lintels and door-posts of the dwellings occupied by the Israelites, that the angel of death passed over, and their first-born remained untouched? Was their temporal salvation secured simply because there was virtue found in the blood of an animal victim? It was because they did exactly what the Lord Jehovah commanded them to do. And that is all we know about it. The Lord has always had a blessing, either temporal or eternal, connected with his positive institutions. The lawyers and doctors, in the days of John the Baptist, "rejected the counsel of God against themselves, by refusing to be baptized by him." On the other hand, the Savior, the peerless and the sinless one, "fulfilled all righteousness" by submitting to the baptism of John. The command of Christ is, "He that believes, and is baptized, shall be saved, and he that believes not [and refuses to be baptized] shall be damned." This is the test law of his kingdom. By this he tries the loyalty of every person who proposes to become a subject of his kingdom. Baptism is an act of obedience, and obedience grows out of respect for the authority of him who is the Head of the Church— the head of all principality and power, and might and dominion.

PROPHECY AND FULFILLMENT.

"And while I was speaking and praying, and confessing my sin, and the sin of my people Israel, and presenting my supplication before the Lord my God, for the holy mountain of my God; yea, while I was speaking in prayer, even the man Gabriel, whom I had seen in the vision at the beginning, being caused to fly swiftly, touched me about the time of evening oblation. And he informed me, and talked with me, and said, "O Daniel, I am now come forth to give thee skill and understanding! At the beginning of thy supplications the commandment came forth, and I am come to show thee; for thou art greatly beloved: therefore understand the matter, and consider the vision.

"Seventy weeks are determined upon thy people and upon thy holy city, to finish the transgression, and to make an end of sins, and to make reconciliation for iniquity, and to bring in everlasting righteousness, and to seal up the vision of the prophecy, and to anoint the Most Holy. Know, therefore, and understand, that from the giving forth of the commandment to restore and to build Jerusalem, unto Messiah the Prince, shall be seven weeks, and threescore and two weeks ; the street shall be built again, and the wall, even in troublous times. And after threescore and two weeks shall Messiah be cut off, but not for himself : and the people of the prince that shall come, shall destroy the city and sanctuary ; and the end thereof shall be with a flood, and unto the end of the war desolations are determined. And he shall confirm the covenant with many for one week ; and in the midst of the week he shall cause the sacrifice and the oblation to cease, and for the overspreading of abominations he shall make it desolate, even until the consummation, and that determined, shall be poured upon the desolate." Daniel ix. 22–27.

The fulfillment of this prophecy is one of the most remarkable phenomena in the history of the world. It is a component part of the divine unity of the Bible. Aided by helps from various sources, we shall proceed to explain it.

The Israelites, in reckoning their time, made use of two kinds of weeks, very different in duration, but the same in parts, commence-

ment and termination. They used the week
so well known with us, seven days in extent,
and beginning with a Sabbath of one day or
twenty-four hours. Their other week, which
we have ceased to use, was seven years in extent, and began with a Sabbath of one year's
duration. Of course each day of this week
was one year. The Israelite who would say it
was three weeks until jubilee, meant twenty-
one years. That a week was seven years in
length, did not seem strange to him, as it does
to those who have long ceased to compute time
in this way. The heathen took up the Jewish
mode, and reckoned by that week. A cel-
ebrated author, in writing his life, and stating
that he had passed his eleventh week, did not
pause to make any explanation. He seemed
to understand the pagan world at that time
were so familiar with the week of years, that
all his readers would know he was seventy-
seven years of age. The peculiar people with
whom Daniel was associated, and perhaps all
the surrounding nations, knew well that these
seventy weeks named by the angel reached
across 490 years ; and they were anticipating
the appearance of a great and triumphant

Savior the very year in which the Christ was
born, but they would not recognize him, because he did not appear in the garb of a prince-
royal, and because he did not come with blaz-
ing pomp and the glorious circumstance of war.

The people of Israel were in captivity ; their
homes were desolate and their lovely land de-
spoiled; and if they ever should return to rebuild their city, it must be by a royal edict
through him who held them in subjection.
After the vision of the prophet, those who were
anxiously watching for the redemption of the
world would also watch and listen for a command from some of the Persian monarchs to
restore and rebuild Jerusalem ; and, from the
date of this royal edict, they would note the
commencement of the seventy weeks.   There
were two edicts to this effect: ordering, and
then ordering again, the restoration of Jerusalem.   One of these decrees was obtained in the
seventh and the other in the twentieth year of
Artaxerxes.

"That the dispersed Jews," remarks the
learned Sir Isaac Newton, "became a people
and a city, when they returned into a *body
politic;* and that was in the seventh year of

Artaxerxes Longimanus." The seventy weeks
accomplish the declarations of Heaven, if begun,
immediately after one of these commandments,
and if weeks of solar years are used; while
from the other, if seventy weeks of lunar years
are counted, the termination is the same. This
astronomical accommodation excites the surprise
of many persons. It is said that the discov-
eries which Sir Isaac Newton stated would be
made from this prophecy, have been seen by
astronomers now alive but the Christian world
have never had, it seems, a plain and satisfac-
tory account of this matter.

Whoever reads the records of Ezra and
Nehemiah, will realize that the difficulties connected with the restoration of Jerusalem were
indeed of such pressing importance as to merit
the language " *troublous times.*" That expression will never again stand before him as
covered with obscurity. Scott, in his valuable
commentary, points us to the fact that the term
of seventy weeks in the text is divided into
three several portions. These three different
periods are of very unequal length; but when
added together, make up the seventy. They
are a term of seven weeks, and of sixty-two

weeks, and of one week. The seven-weeks term extends across the time of building, which was characterized by so much toil and danger. This lasted *forty-nine* years: each one of the seven weeks being seven years, according to our mode of reckoning. So persecuted were the workmen, that while using the trowel with one hand they were obliged to defend themselves with a sword in the other. The sixty-two weeks seem to extend from this time until the Most Holy was anointed on the sacred banks of the Jordan. Oil had been used to anoint the Jewish high priests; but the Messiah was anointed with the Holy Spirit, which descended in the form of a dove and rested upon his person. After his baptism, the Savior traveled and preached, and performed many miracles, for three years and six months (just the half of a week) before he was crucified. He arose from the dead, and, after commissioning his Apostles to go preach the gospel, beginning at Jerusalem, he ascended into heaven. They went; and, during another half week, many thousands accepted the conditions of the New Covenant, and to whom the covenant was confirmed, before the ambassadors of Jesus Christ

were driven from Jerusalem and Judea to make
proclamation to the Gentiles.   This last term
of one week is divided into two parts.   It was
in the middle of it that the great Sacrifice was
offered, which once and forever destroyed the
efficacy of all other sacrifices.   It was in the
middle of the week that the oblation was
poured out, which instantly cut off the meri-
torious effects of a l other oblations.   We are
informed that at the time when the Messiah
should be cut off, the sacrifice would not be
made in his own behalf.   This fact points to
the atonement—to the vicarious sufferings of
the Savior—which had been typified upon
Jewish altars for a thousand yea s, and which
had been made prominent in the glowing prophetic words of Isaiah and other prophets.

During the three years and a half before the
death of Christ, he, with his Apostles, confirmed this covenant with many of Daniel's
nation; and his Apostles, after he left them,
did the same for half a week in his name.
After this, obstinacy prevailed; and it was not
very long before the "*people of the prince*,"
that was foretold when Daniel lived (the
Romans), came as the eagles fly, and did destroy

"the *city* and the *sanctuary*." If any one should inquire what is meant by the sentence, *the end thereof shall be with a flood*, we answer by asking him to read a full account of the siege and destruction of Jerusalem. Flavius Josephus was a spectator of that flood; consult his history. As regards the desolations which were to overwhelm the nation that "cut off" the Messiah, we are only told that they should march on (as a people, but not *as a nation*) until the final consummation. God's interested people have seen them pouring out, and have looked on with wonder for eighteen centuries, asking "*Will this torrent never cease to beat upon the desolate?*" The answer is, *Not before* the consummation, which even now may be near at hand.

Twelve verses in the 53d chapter of Isaiah contain an accurate representation of the life, reception, character, trial, manner of trial, death, manner of death, resurrection, etc., of the crucified Savior. The fulfillment of the prophecies contained in this chapter, as they center in the person of Christ, is a moral miracle of such magnitude, that the infidel world have never attempted its solution. It is an impassable barrier to all their vain conceits, and stands as a pyramid of truth which they never can undermine with the keenest edges of speculative philosophy.

The evangelical prophet, by anticipation, submits the question, " Who hath believed our report, and to whom is the arm of the Lord revealed?" The humiliation of the Savior to the proud and arrogant Jews was a "report" they were unwilling to believe. But the wonder of the "report" consists in the fact that he was "found of a people [the Gentiles] who sought not after him."

"He shall grow up before him as a tender plant, and as a root out of dry ground." Plants that grow from a dry soil are tender, and require more watering and a closer care of the gardener than others. The Redeemer of the world was waited on by the angels of heaven; he was strengthened when he was the weakest, encouraged when he was the faintest, and heard when he was in despair. He was a tender plant in the eyes of his heavenly Father. He disappointed the expectation of the Jews, because these words of the prophet were fulfilled in their presence: "He hath no form nor comeliness, and when we shall see him, there is no beauty that we shall desire him." Instead of gazing on an imperial prince, who would come with the pageantry of Oriental kings to deliver the Jewish nation from Roman bondage, and who would establish an empire of earthly glory, the descendants of David and Solomon could only look upon him who was born in a stable and cradled in a manger, who took upon himself the form of a servant, who worked at the carpenter's bench with his brethren, and who was regarded by his neighbors as only the reputed son of Joseph of Nazareth.

" He is despised and rejected of men, a man of sorrows and acquainted with grief; and we hid as it were our faces from him. He was despised, and we esteemed him not. Surely he hath born our griefs, and carried our sorrows; yet we did esteem him stricken, smitten of God and afflicted. But he was wounded for our transgressions ; he was bruised for our iniquities; the chastisement of our peace was upon him, and with his stripes we are healed. All we like sheep have gone astray, we have turned every one to his own way, and the Lord hath laid on him the iniquity of us all." In these wonderful words, which seem to be an echo from the eternal world, and which have ever since reverberated through successive ages, we discover the doctrine which contains the ideas of sin, sacrifice, reconciliation, substitution, etc.

According to the Mishna and other Jewish authorities, it was customary among the Jews, that when any one was on trial for a capital offense, proclamation was made, with the understanding that if any person knew anything of the prisoner's innocence, he should come forward and declare the fact; but no such proclamation was made on the trial of Jesus. Jesus was silent in the presence of Pilate. Criminals usually, when taken into custody, are confined in the jail until the setting of the court, which does not commence for weeks and months. If they are tried and condemned, they are thrown again into prison, and after a time executed. Unlike the manner of disposing of criminals in the usual legal process, Jesus was taken into custody, and hurried directly before the judgment-seat; his trial hurried by shouts of impatience, and, as soon as condemned, he was taken from judgment immediately to the place of execution.

"He made his grave with the wicked, and with the rich in his death, because he had done no violence, neither was any deceit in his mouth." The fact is recorded by the evangelists that his body was laid in the new tomb of the rich man of Arimathea, where it was guarded by the wicked Roman soldiery. Some Hebrew scholars assert that according to the original test, as stated in the New Testament, they designed his grave with the wicked ; but God ordered it otherwise, because he had done no violence ; because he was not a malefactor, he was not permitted to be buried with malefactors, where his enemies were certainly about to bury him, if no one had asked Pilate for his body.

"Yet it pleased the Lord to bruise him, he hath put him to grief ; when thou shalt make his soul an offering for sin, he shall see his seed, he shall prolong his days, and the pleasure of the Lord shall prosper in his hands." Though "cut off out of the land of the living," yet his days were to be prolonged, which fact was verified by his resurrection from the dead.

After his resurrection and ascension, he established his Church, since which time millions of souls have come under his peaceful reign, and the pleasure of the Lord prospers in his hands by the extension of his kingdom "from the river to the ends of the earth."

"He shall see of the travail of his soul, and shall be satisfied; by his knowledge shall my righteous servant justify many, for he shall bear their iniquities. Therefore will I divide him a portion with the great, and he shall divide the spoil with the strong, because he hath poured out his soul unto death; and he was numbered with the transgressors, and he bare the sins of many, and made intercession for the transgressors." The Oriental expression of having a portion with the great, and dividing the spoil with the strong, according to other eastern authorities, referred to *prosperity*. Surely his "portion" has become truly great, for, at his coronation, on his throne of glory, God said: "Ask of me, and I will give thee the heathen for thine inheritance, and the uttermost parts of the earth for thy possession." The doctrine of *vicarious sufferings* is repeated in these last two verses. That he was to be numbered with actual transgressors is declared —one was crucified on his right hand, and the other on his left. In harmony with his pure and peerless character, his expiring prayer on the accursed cross was in behalf of his murderers and betrayers, when he said, "Father, forgive them, they know not what they do."

The seed of the woman was to bruise the serpent's head. Genesis iii. 15. The seed of the woman is Christ. The serpent is Satan. Christ delivers from the bondage of death. Hebrews ii. 15.

A star appeared over the birthplace of the Savior. Balaam predicted that "there shall come a Star out of Jacob, and a Sceptre shall rise out of Israel." Numbers xxiv. 17. The coincidence is remarkable.

Moses foretold that Christ would appear as a great prophet. "The Lord thy God will raise up unto thee a Prophet from the midst of thy brethren, like unto me : to him shall you hearken." Deut. xviii. 15.

Jacob predicted that "the Sceptre shall not depart from Judah, nor a lawgiver from between his feet [from among his descendants], until Shiloh come ; and unto him shall the gathering of the people be." Genesis xlix. 10.

Isaiah predicted that the Messiah should be born of a virgin. "Therefore the Lord himself shall give you a *sign*. Behold, a virgin shall conceive, and bear a son, and shall call his name Immanuel." Isaiah vii. 14.

Look at these wonderful words of the same prophet : "For unto us a child is born, unto us a son is given ; and the government shall be upon his shoulder ; and his name shall be called *Wonderful Counselor, the Mighty God, the Everlasting Father, the Prince of Peace.* Of the increase of his government and peace there shall be no end, upon the throne of David, and upon his kingdom, to order it, and to establish it, with judgment and justice from henceforth even forever." Isaiah ix. 6, 7.

Concerning the pedigree of Christ, as " the Stem of Jesse," and as a " Branch " of the house of David, and concerning his spirit of wisdom and understanding, read the eleventh chapter of Isaiah. The joyful flourishing of Christ's kingdom, with the superlative privileges of the gospel, are described in the thirty-fifth chapter.

The prophet Micah predicts the birthplace of Jesus. "And thou, Bethlehem Ephratah, though thou be little [or the least] among the thousands of Judah, yet out of these shall he come forth unto me, that is to be ruler in Israel; whose goings forth have been from of old, from everlasting." This was literally fulfilled, as may be seen by reading Matthew ii. 6.

The anointing of Christ by the Holy Spirit, and his mission to the captive poor, are graphically described in the sixty-first chapter of Isaiah.

The scenes that transpired around the cross, the taunts of the Jewish rabble, and the mockeries of the Roman soldiers, are portrayed in the twenty-second Psalm.

His triumphant entrance into the courts of glory is thus described in the twenty-fourth Psalm :

"Lift up your heads, O ye gates; and be ye lifted up, ye everlasting doors; and the King of Glory shall come in. Who is this

King of Glory? The Lord strong and mighty; the Lord mighty in battle. Lift up your heads, O ye gates; even lift them up, ye everlasting doors, and the King of Glory shall come in. Who is this King of Glory? The Lord of host, she is the King of Glory."